Employers are responsible for providing a safe and healthful workplace for their employees. OSHA's role is to assure the safety and health of America's workers by setting and enforcing standards; providing training, outreach and education; establishing partnerships; and encouraging continual improvement in workplace safety and health.

This handbook provides a general overview of a particular topic related to OSHA standards. It does not alter or determine compliance responsibilities in OSHA standards or the *Occupational Safety and Health Act of 1970.* Because interpretations and enforcement policy may change over time, you should consult current OSHA administrative interpretations and decisions by the Occupational Safety and Health Review Commission and the Courts for additional guidance on OSHA compliance requirements.

This information is available to sensory impaired individuals upon request. Voice phone: (202) 693-1999; teletypewriter (TTY) number: (877) 889-5627.

Reducing Worker Exposure to
Perchloroethylene (PERC) in Dry Cleaning

U.S. Department of Labor

Occupational Safety and Health Administration

OSHA 3253-05N
2005

Contents

Executive Summary

This document has been prepared by the Occupational Safety and Health Administration (OSHA) to help dry cleaning establishments reduce employee exposures to perchloroethylene (also known as perc, tetrachloroethylene, C_2Cl_4 or $Cl_2C=CCl_2$). The dry cleaning industry has improved the control of perchloroethylene in recent years, and modern dry cleaning equipment involves much lower exposures than older style equipment. However, there is still a need to reduce employee exposure to the chemical to reduce any possible health effects that could result from long-term exposure to the chemical.

Many dry cleaning employers have found that equipment design, preventive maintenance, control of leaks in equipment, proper ventilation, and good work practices can reduce perc exposure to workers, reduce costs by recovering perc for reuse, help create a cleaner environment, and help comply with federal and state environmental regulations.

This booklet is not a standard or regulation, and it creates no new legal obligations. The document is advisory in nature, informational in content, and is intended to assist employers in providing a safe and healthful workplace. The *Occupational Safety and Health Act* requires employers to comply with hazard-specific safety and health standards. In addition, pursuant to Section 5(a)(1), the General Duty Clause of the Act, employers must provide their employees with a workplace free from recognized hazards likely to cause death or serious physical harm. Employers can be cited for violating the General Duty Clause if there is a recognized hazard and they do not take reasonable steps to prevent or abate the hazard. However, failure to implement these recommendations is not, in itself, a violation of the General Duty Clause. Citations can only be based on standards, regulations, and the General Duty Clause.

Introduction

Perchloroethylene ("perc") has long been recognized as an effective dry cleaning solvent and today it is by far the most commonly used solvent in dry cleaning shops. However, as a volatile organic solvent, perc may pose serious health hazards if exposure is not properly controlled. Dry cleaning workers who routinely breathe excessive amounts of the solvent vapor or spill perc on their skin are at risk of developing health problems.

Special precautions are recommended to avoid health risks from perc exposure. The purpose of this guidance is to provide practical and effective ways for dry cleaning operators to reduce worker exposure to perc. The guidance emphasizes reducing perc exposure through a combination of using modern equipment and preventive maintenance, control of leaks in dry cleaning equipment, proper ventilation, and good work practices.

Health Hazards

During dry cleaning, perc primarily enters the body from inhalation of the vapors, potentially resulting in the following health hazards:

- Dizziness, drowsiness, and loss of coordination;
- Mild loss of memory, visual perception, and reaction time after several years of exposure; or
- Redness and blistering of the skin after prolonged dermal contact.

There is some evidence of an association between perc and increased risk of certain cancers in dry cleaning workers exposed for many years. The National Institute for Occupational Safety and Health (NIOSH) has designated perc as a "potential occupational carcinogen." The National Toxicology Program has designated it as "reasonably anticipated to be a human carcinogen." The International Agency for Research on Cancer (IARC) has designated perc as a "probable human carcinogen."

The possibility of these health hazards can be minimized by reducing worker exposures to perc vapor and by avoiding skin contact with perc.

Perc Exposure

Primary Sources of Perc Exposure

Dry cleaning employees may be exposed to perc while performing both routine tasks and machine maintenance. Activities that result in elevated exposure include the following:

- Loading dirty clothes into the machine (when perc-contaminated air is displaced and forced out of the machine);
- Removing clothes, especially thick items, before the drying cycle is finished;
- For transfer machines, transferring solvent-laden clothes into the dryer;
- Cleaning lint and button traps;
- Raking out the still (distillation unit residue);
- Changing the solvent filter;
- Maintenance of water separator; and
- Handling and storage of hazardous waste.

Machine Fugitive Emissions

Uncontrolled emissions, so-called "fugitive emissions," from dry cleaning machines can also expose workers to high levels of perc. These include:

- Perc emissions not captured by vapor recovery and thus released when the loading door is opened or through the vent; and
- Perc emissions from leaks in machines, hoses, valves, and ducts.

Secondary Sources of Perc Exposure

Other possible sources of perc exposure not directly associated with the dry cleaning equipment include:

- Pressing freshly dry-cleaned clothes;

- Using a perc-based spotting agent; and
- Using a perc-based waterproofing agent.[1]

Current Regulations and Recommendations

OSHA has set mandatory permissible exposure limits (PELs) for perc, presented in Table 1. This table also lists perc exposure limits *recommended* by other safety and health organizations.

Table 1.	Worker Exposure Limits for Perchloroethylene (Tetrachloroethylene)	
Organization	8-hour time-weighted average (TWA)	Other limits
OSHA (mandatory)	Permissible Exposure Limit (PEL): 100 parts per million (ppm)	Ceiling: 200 ppm (for 5 mins. in any 3-hr. period), with a maximum peak of 300 ppm
ACGIH (voluntary)	Threshold Limit Value (TLV): 25 ppm	Short-term exposure limit (STEL): 100 ppm (as a 15-min. TWA)
NIOSH	Potential Occupational Carcinogen; Minimize workplace exposure concentrations.	

[1] Use of perc-based spotting or waterproofing agents is not current practice in the dry cleaning industry. However, these operations are addressed in this document for those few dry cleaning establishments that may continue to use these products.

Other OSHA standards that may apply when workers are exposed to perc include: Hazard Communication (29 CFR 1910.1200); General requirements for personal protective equipment (29 CFR 1910.132); and Respiratory Protection (29 CFR 1910.134).

In addition to these worker exposure limits, dry cleaning facilities must comply with EPA regulations controlling the release of perc into the environment – air, land, and water. EPA has developed regulations that affect many aspects of dry cleaning operations, including machine operation and maintenance, building design and ventilation, work practices, as well as perc storage and disposal. There are also EPA requirements on air monitoring for perc release, recordkeeping, and perc use reporting. (For further information on EPA regulations, see *Plain English Guide for Perc Cleaners*, EPA, 2003.)

Machine Design and Maintenance

Dry cleaning technology has evolved substantially over the decades. The newer machine designs (dry-to-dry, closed looped) greatly reduce the amount of perc vapor released into the air inside the shop as well as outdoors, resulting in cost savings since more perc is recovered for reuse, as well as safer working conditions and a cleaner environment.

The oldest type of dry cleaning machines – *transfer* machines – can expose workers to high amounts of perc, particularly during transfer of solvent-laden clothing from washer to dryer. Newer equipment (*dry-to-dry* machines) reduces worker exposure by eliminating this transfer step (clothes enter and exit the machine dry).

The first dry-to-dry equipment, dry-to-dry *vented*, exhausts residual solvent vapors either directly outside or first through a perc vapor recovery system. The present designs, dry-to-dry *closed loop* machines, recirculate perc rather than release it outdoors. The

latest technology incorporates a secondary vapor recovery system on the dry-to-dry *closed loop machines* that most effectively minimizes perc usage, environmental releases, and worker exposure to perc. Figure 1, below, illustrates the perc exposure levels of machine operators associated with the various dry cleaning machines.

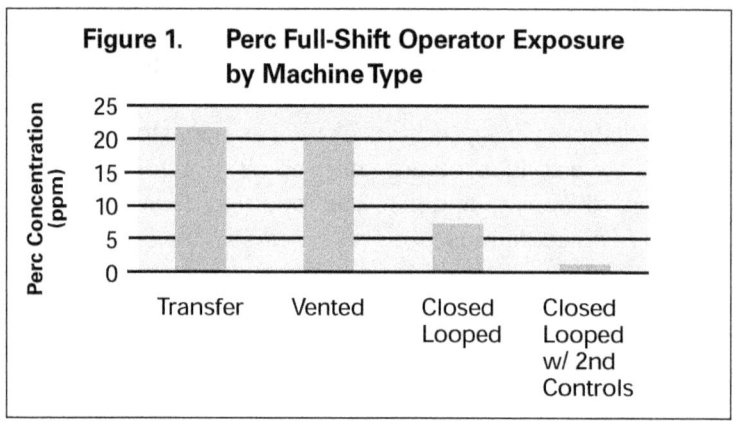

Figure 1. Perc Full-Shift Operator Exposure by Machine Type

Source: NIOSH.

Replacing equipment that wears out with modern equipment can reduce exposures. Also, routine machine maintenance combined with detection and timely repair of identified leaks can be extremely effective in controlling airborne levels of perc vapor. (See the Case Studies starting on page 14.) The EPA estimates that as much as 25 percent of solvent emissions can be attributed to leaks. In addition to creating unsafe airborne levels of perc, leaks are waste-ful and costly. Routine machine maintenance needs to be performed to ensure optimal operation of all components. Appropriate personal protective equipment (PPE) needs to be worn during maintenance activities to ensure protection from perc hazards. (See page 10 for more information on PPE.)

Recommended machine maintenance activities include the following:

- Clean lint and button traps regularly to prevent clogging of condensers and fans.

- Rake out still daily. (Consider installing a pump that allows residue to be pumped directly to a safety can.)
- Change all filters as necessary.
- Desorb carbon adsorber before saturation point.
- Adjust refrigerated condensers to ensure proper temperature of drying air.
- Maintain and repair exhaust fans.

A recommended schedule of maintenance activities is provided in Appendix A at pages 16 -17.

NEVER PERFORM MAINTENANCE WHILE DRY CLEANING EQUIPMENT IS OPERATING.

To control perc leaks from dry cleaning equipment:

- Perform daily checks for leaks in door gaskets, valves, hoses, pumps, tubing, and piping connections. Look for liquid pools and droplets on or around equipment. Unusual solvent odor may indicate a vapor leak (do not rely only on the sense of smell for detecting leaks).
- Replace gaskets before they become hard, cracked, or worn.
- Use a direct-reading air-monitoring device (see page 13) to detect vapor leaks in piping, exhaust ductwork, and associated components.
- Use perc-resistant seals and fittings recommended by the manufacturer of the machine.
- Repair leaks immediately.

Ventilation

Adequate ventilation is essential for controlling perc levels within the dry cleaning shop. *General ventilation*, provided by equipment such as overhead fans, is useful for reducing heat and humidity, and diluting perc levels. Such ventilation can be designed to move the perc vapors away from workers and customers while continuously supplying clean, fresh air to the dry cleaning area.

Local exhaust ventilation (LEV) captures perc vapor at the source of the release, removing the vapor before it enters the air inside the shop. Well-designed LEV may be provided where perc exposure is highest, for example, at the loading door. Newer dry cleaning equipment has built-in LEV designed to prevent escape of vapors during machine loading and unloading. For machines without built-in LEV, an external ventilation hood outside the machine door can be installed to control vapors when the door is open. (A study describing this method of control is summarized in Case Study #5 at page 16.)

Detailed information regarding desirable configurations for general ventilation and LEV as well as recommendations on exhaust fan placement and capacity can be found in pamphlets by the International Fabricare Institute (IFI) (1989)[2] and NIOSH (1998)[3].

PPE, Work Practices and Training

Personal protective equipment (PPE) – including aprons, gloves, goggles, and respirators approved for use with organic chemicals – is used to help workers avoid perc exposure. Workers must wear respirators **equipped with filters or cartridges specifically designed for organic vapors** when elevated perc exposures are anticipated (29 CFR 1919.134). Tasks where elevated exposure may occur include

[2] IFI. 1989. Reducing Vapor Exposure: OSHA compliance. International Fabricare Institute. Vol. 13, No. 5.

[3] NIOSH. 1998. Control of Exposure to Perchloroethylene in Commercial Drycleaning. NIOSH Hazard Controls. DHHS (NIOSH) Publication No. 97-154. http://www.cdc.gov/niosh/hc16.html

machine maintenance, filter changes, waterproofing operations, and loading/unloading machines (depending on the equipment in use). Workers using transfer machines may also need to wear chemical-resistant aprons. Spotters can wear goggles, chemical-resistant aprons, and gloves. Spill cleanup workers always need to wear respirators and gloves.

Work Practices – Good work practices can greatly minimize worker exposure to perc vapors. For example, peak exposure levels can be reduced by several hundred parts per million simply by proper positioning of the worker's head and body during transfer operations. Other important work practices to reduce perc exposures are listed below.

Work Practice Tips for Dry Cleaning Operators

- Do not load the machine past its capacity.
- Do not open the machine door when the cycle is running.
- Keep the machine door CLOSED as much as possible.
- Do not "shortcut" the drying cycle by removing garments from the machine before the cycle is finished.
- Keep your head and face turned away from the machine door and clothes when removing solvent-laden clothes from the washer.
- Do not transfer perc to machines by hand or with open buckets. Use a closed piping system that connects directly to the machine drum.
- WAIT until the machine and solvent are cold before performing maintenance.
- Use spotting agents sparingly.
- Use perc-free spotting agents.
- Clean up perc spills immediately. (The shop should have in place a plan for safely responding to perc spills.)
- Store containers of perc and perc wastes in tightly sealed containers.
- Position your hand away from the door when opening a transfer machine.

Training – Dry cleaning employees need training on how to protect themselves from the hazards of perc (OSHA Hazard Communication standard, 29 CFR 1910.1200). Employees should be trained in proper work practices for all of their expected tasks – operating and maintaining machines, spotting, waterproofing, housekeeping, and perc transfer and storage.

Workers must be trained on the health hazards and symptoms associated with perc exposure. Workers should become familiar with Material Safety Data Sheets (MSDS) and container labels for perc (OSHA Hazard Communication standard, 29 CFR 1910.1200). The International Chemical Safety Card for perc can be found in Appendix B on pages 18-20 of this publication to help with this training.

In addition, workers should be familiar with the location and proper use of eyewash stations as well as procedures for responding to first aid emergencies, such as eye splashes and skin contamination. OSHA requires employers to train their employees about hazards and methods to prevent exposure to chemicals used in the workplace (OSHA Hazard Communication standard, 29 CFR 1910.1200). Workers must also be trained on the proper use of respirators (Respiratory Protection standard, 29 CFR 1910.134).

Perc Air Monitoring

A variety of devices and instruments are available to measure perc levels in the air. Reasons for performing air monitoring include:

- To determine the perc exposure levels of individual employees;
- To identify sources of leaks in equipment; and
- To measure perc levels before and after modifications to equipment or procedures.

The type of air monitoring method used depends on the purpose of the sampling, the technical abilities of the person who conducts the testing, and the cost of the equipment. To determine

the perc exposures of individual workers, a sample can be obtained by clipping a monitoring device to the worker's collar either with a battery-powered pump or a simple monitoring badge.

The samples are then sent to a qualified laboratory to analyze the perc concentration. The results can be compared with the OSHA PEL and other recommended exposure limits for perc (listed in Table 1, on page 6).

For detecting equipment leaks and other emissions, portable, direct-reading devices provide either a visual/audible indication of a leak or an instantaneous measurement of the perc vapor concentration at the source of the emission. These instruments vary in terms of cost, accuracy, and ease of use.

Two relatively inexpensive, easy to use leak-detection devices are:

- Small, hand-held refrigerant leak detectors that indicate a perc leak by a visual and audible signal; and
- Colorimetric detector tubes (used with small, hand-operated pumps) that change color depending on the perc vapor concentration.

More sophisticated types of direct reading devices include infrared analyzers and photoionization detectors that provide accurate measurements of perc concentration, but are more expensive and require technical expertise to operate.

Assistance

OSHA has a free consultation service for small and medium-sized businesses with hazardous operations. The service is confidential and offers the expertise of qualified occupational safety and health professionals to employers who request advice and assistance. OSHA consultation is available in all 50 States, the District of Columbia, Guam, Puerto Rico, the Northern Mariana Islands and the Virgin Islands. Information on OSHA consultation services can be found at:
www.osha.gov/dcsp/smallbusiness/consult.html

For assistance with perc monitoring, consult your perc supplier's product stewardship program or a professional dry cleaning association, such as the International Fabricare Institute. If you need the technical expertise of an industrial hygienist, the American Industrial Hygiene Association (AIHA) offers a listing of qualified consultants at: http://www.aiha.org/ConsultantsConsumers/html/consultants client.asp

Case Studies

Dry cleaning shop owners have numerous options available for reducing the perc exposures of their employees. The case studies below describe the effectiveness of measures such as installing relatively low-cost machine retrofits, installing LEV, and performing routine machine maintenance and leak detection.

Case Study #1: Emission Control Retrofit – Carbon Adsorber

Installing a new carbon adsorber on a dry cleaning machine reduced the perc exposures of operators by 92 percent, according to a NIOSH study. The 60-pound, closed-loop carbon adsorber was installed to remove residual perc not collected by the existing re-frigerated condenser on the closed-loop, dry-to-dry machine. The retrofit cost less than $5,000.

Before the retrofit, the average perc exposure of operators during the one-minute machine loading and unloading process was 353 ppm. After the carbon adsorber was installed, the average exposure was 29 ppm, a reduction of approximately 92 percent.

Case Study #2: Emission Control Retrofit – Refrigerated Condenser

A NIOSH study found that perc exposures of dry cleaning machine operators were reduced by 60 percent after a refriger-ated condenser was installed on a dry cleaning machine.

A 5-ton cooling capacity refrigerated condenser was installed on a vented, dry-to-dry machine in place of its original water-cooled condenser and single-pass carbon adsorber. The retrofit cost less than $5,000. Before the installation of the refrigerated condenser, the average perc exposure of machine operators during the one-minute machine loading and unloading phase was 1,139 ppm. After the retrofit, the average exposure was 456 ppm, a reduction of about 60 percent. NIOSH cautioned that only dry cleaning machines in good repair with few leaks should be considered for retrofitting. Although this technology significantly reduced perc exposure in this case, it does not eliminate it and additional controls would be needed to achieve further reductions.

Case Study #3: Gasket Leak – Detection and Repair

Repairing a leaking gasket on a dry cleaning machine resulted in a full-shift perc exposure reduction of 22 ppm, according to a NIOSH study of retrofit emission controls (described further in Case Study #2). The gasket at the rear of the machine being retrofitted with a new refrigerated condenser sprung a leak during the installation. Before the retrofit, TWA perc concentrations averaged 47 ppm. Measurements taken after the leak was fixed resulted in an average perc exposure of 25 ppm.

Case Study #4: Distillation Unit Leak – Detection and Repair

During the LEV evaluation (described in Case Study #5), NIOSH noted that the full-shift perc exposures of machine operators were up to four times higher on the day when the distillation unit was operating (about 20 ppm vs. 5 ppm when the unit was turned off). These elevated readings led to the identification and repair of a leak in the distillation system. If perc monitoring had not been conducted, the leak might not have been detected. This study underscores the importance of routine perc air monitoring to identify and repair equipment leaks.

Case Study #5: Local Exhaust Ventilation

A NIOSH study showed that installation of a simple, inexpensive LEV system was effective in reducing average full-shift TWA perc exposures of machine operators by 37 percent.

Before the LEV installation, the average full-shift perc exposure was 4.7 ppm. The 12-year-old dry cleaning machine was a dry-to-dry, closed-loop design with a 50-pound capacity. The LEV system, including fabrication, installation, and electric wiring, was installed for $2,560. The LEV was positioned directly above the dry cleaning machine door and exhausted air from in front of the door only when the door was opened. The average perc exposure was reduced by about 37 percent, to 3.0 ppm, after the LEV installation.

Appendix A

Recommended Maintenance Schedule for Dry Cleaning Machines

Daily Maintenance Tasks

- Clean button trap strainer and lint bag.
- Dispose of contaminated water from the water separator.
- Desorb the carbon adsorber.
- Rake out the still of the distillation unit (or weekly as needed).

Weekly Maintenance Tasks*

- Check door seatings and gaskets of machine cylinder for liquid and vapor leaks.
- Check the button trap for lid leaks.
- Launder the lint bag.
- Check seals and gaskets of the refrigerated condenser's diverter valve, distillation unit, filters, filter housings, and muck cooker for liquid and vapor leaks.

- Rake out the still of the distillation unit (or daily as needed).
- Clean the separator tank of the water separator and perform leak checks.
- Measure the exhaust temperature of the refrigerated condenser.
- Measure perc in the exhaust system.
- Perform leak checks on hose and pipe connections, fittings, couplings, and valves.

Monthly Maintenance Tasks

- Check the exhaust damper (vented machines) for liquid and vapor leaks.
- Check for lint buildup on the heating and condensing coils and refrigerated condenser coils.
- Check for leaks in the ductwork of the lint trap and carbon adsorber.
- Check for lint buildup on the temperature probe of the lint trap.
- Clean the vent of the water separator.

Semi-Annual Maintenance Tasks

- Clean the muck cooker's steam and condensation coils.

Annual Maintenance Tasks

- Clean the heating/condensing and refrigerated condenser coils.

Other

- Clean and change filters according to the manufacturer's schedule.

*Note: The EPA requires weekly leak detection and repair for large dry cleaners and bimonthly leak detection and repair for small dry cleaners. The type of machine (dry-to-dry or transfer) and the amount of perc purchased each year determines whether a dry cleaner is large or small. Refer to the *Plain English Guide for Perc Cleaners* for details (http://www.epa.gov/opptintr/dfe/pubs/garment/perc/).

Appendix B

International Chemical Safety Card for Tetrachloroethylene

The following International Chemical Safety Card (ICSC) for tetrachloroethylene was published in 2000. The ICSCs project is an undertaking of the International Programme on Chemical Safety (IPCS). The project is being developed in cooperation between the IPCS and the Commission of the European Communities. The IPCS is a joint activity of three cooperating international organizations: the United Nations Environment Programme (UNEP), the International Labour Office (ILO) and the World Health Organization (WHO). The main objective of the IPCS is to carry out and disseminate evaluations of the hazards posed by chemicals to human health and the environment.

ICSC cards summarize essential health and safety information on chemicals for their use at the shop floor level by workers and employers. Cards are available for over 1,300 chemicals, and they are provided in several languages, including English, Korean, Spanish, Russian, French, German, Japanese and Chinese.

To access the most recent ICSC card for perc, to locate the perc card in another language, or to find the card for another chemical, access the NIOSH Internet site at: http://www.cdc.gov/niosh/ipcsneng/neng0076.html.

TETRACHLOROETHYLENE

ICSC: 0076

1,1,2,2-Tetrachloroethylene
Perchloroethylene
Tetrachloroethene
C_2Cl_4 / $Cl_2C=CCl_2$
Molecular mass: 165.8

ICSC #   0076
CAS #   127-18-4
RTECS #   KX3850000
UN #   1897
EC #   602-028-00-4

TYPES OF HAZARD/ EXPOSURE	ACUTE HAZARDS/SYMPTOMS	PREVENTION	FIRST AID/ FIRE FIGHTING
FIRE	Not combustible. Gives off iritating or toxic fumes (or gases) in a fire.		In case of fire in the surroundings: all extinguishing agents allowed.
EXPLOSION			
EXPOSURE		STRICT HYGIENE! PREVENT GENERATION OF MISTS!	
• INHALATION	Dizziness. Drowsiness. Headache. Nausea. Weakness. Unconsciousness.	Ventilation, local exhaust, or breathing protection.	Fresh air, rest. Artificial respiration if indicated. Refer for medical attention.
• SKIN	Dry skin. Redness.	Protective gloves. Protective clothing.	Remove contaminated clothes. Rinse and then wash skin with water and soap.
• EYES	Redness. Pain.	Safety googles, face shield.	First rinse with plenty of water for several minutes (remove contact lenses if easily possible), then take to a doctor.
• INGESTION	Abdominal pain (further see Inhalation).	Do not eat, drink, or smoke during work.	Rinse mouth. DO NOT induce vomiting. Give plenty of water to drink. Rest.

SPILLAGE DISPOSAL	STORAGE	PACKAGING & LABELLING
Ventilation. Collect leaking and spilled liquid in sealable containers as far as possible. Absorb remaining liquid in sand or inert absorbent and remove to safe place. Do NOT let this chemical enter the environment. (Extra personal protection: filter respirator for organic gases and vapours).	Separated from metals (see Chemical Dangers), food and feedstuffs. Keep in the dark. Ventilation along the floor.	Do not transport with food and feedstuffs. Marine pollutant. Xn symbol N symbol R: 40-51/53 S: (2-)23-36/37-61 UN Hazard Class: 6.1 UN Packing Group: III

SEE IMPORTANT INFORMATION ON BACK

ICSC: 0076

Prepared in the context of cooperation between the International Programme on Chemical Safety & the Commission of the European Communities (C) IPCS CEC 2001. No modifications to the International version have been made except to add the OSHA PELs, NIOSH RELs and NIOSH IDLH values.

TETRACHLOROETHYLENE

ICSC: 0076

I M P O R T A N T D A T A	**PHYSICAL STATE; APPEARANCE:** COLOURLESS LIQUID, WITH CHARACTERISTIC ODOUR.

PHYSICAL STATE; APPEARANCE:
COLOURLESS LIQUID, WITH CHARACTERISTIC ODOUR.

PHYSICAL DANGERS:
The vapor is heavier than air.

CHEMICAL DANGERS:
On contact with hot surfaces or flames this substance decomposes forming toxic and corrosive fumes (hydrogen chloride, phosgene, chlorine). The substance decomposes slowly on contact with moisture producing trichloroacetic acid and hydrochloric acid. Reacts with metals such as aluminum, lithium, barium, beryllium.

OCCUPATIONAL EXPOSURE LIMITS:
TLV: 25 ppm; RET(STEL): 100 ppm; (ACGIH 1999).
OSHA PEL: TWA 100 ppm C 200 ppm 300 ppm (5-minute maximum peak in any 3-hours)
NIOSH REL: Ca Minimize workplace exposure concentrations. See Appendix A.
NIOSH IDLH: Potential occupational carcinogen 150 ppm.

ROUTES OF EXPOSURE:
The substance can be absorbed into the body by inhalation and by ingestion.

INHALATION RISK:
A harmful contamination of the air will be reached rather slowly on evaporation of this substance at 20°C.

EFFECTS OF SHORT-TERM EXPOSURE:
The substance irritates the eyes, the skin and the respiratory tract. Swallowing the liquid may cause aspiration into the lungs with the risk of chemical pneumonitis. The substance may cause effects on the central nervous system. Exposure at high levels may result in unconsciousness.

EFFECTS OF LONG-TERM OR REPEATED EXPOSURE:
Repeated or prolonged contact with skin may cause dermatitis. The substance may have effects on the liver and kidneys. This substance is probably carcinogenic to humans.

PHYSICAL PROPERTIES	Boiling point: 121°C Melting point: -22°C Relative density (water = 1): 1.6 Solubility in water, g/100 ml at 20°C: 0.015	Vapour pressure, kPa at 20°C: 1.9 Relative vapour density (air = 1): 5.8 Relative density of the vapour/air-mixture at 20°C (air = 1): 1.09 Octanol/water partition coefficient as log Pow: 2.9

Boiling point: 121°C
Melting point: -22°C
Relative density (water = 1): 1.6
Solubility in water, g/100 ml at 20°C: 0.015

Vapour pressure, kPa at 20°C: 1.9
Relative vapour density (air = 1): 5.8
Relative density of the vapour/air-mixture at 20°C (air = 1): 1.09
Octanol/water partition coefficient as log Pow: 2.9

ENVIRONMENTAL DATA	The substance is toxic to aquatic organisms. The substance may cause long-term effects in the aquatic environment.

NOTES

Depending on the degree of exposure, periodic medical examination is indicated. The odour warning when the exposure limit value is exceeded is insufficient. Do NOT use in the vicinity of a fire or a hot surface, or during welding. An added stabilizer or inhibitor can influence the toxicological properties of this substance, consult an expert.

Transport Emergency Card: TEC (R)-722
NFPA Code: H2; FO; RO;

ADDITIONAL INFORMATION

ICSC: 0076   TETRACHLOROETHYLENE

OSHA Assistance

OSHA can provide extensive help through a variety of programs, including technical assistance about effective safety and health programs, state plans, workplace consultations, voluntary protection programs, strategic partnerships, training and education, and more. An overall commitment to workplace safety and health can add value to your business, to your workplace and to your life.

Safety and Health Program Management Guidelines

Effective management of worker safety and health protection is a decisive factor in reducing the extent and severity of work-related injuries and illnesses and their related costs. In fact, an effective safety and health program forms the basis of good worker protection and can save time and money (about $4 for every dollar spent) and increase productivity and reduce worker injuries, illnesses and related workers' compensation costs.

To assist employers and employees in developing effective safety and health programs, OSHA published recommended *Safety and Health Program Management Guidelines* (54 *Federal Register* (16): 3904-3916, January 26, 1989). These voluntary guidelines apply to all places of employment covered by OSHA.

The guidelines identify four general elements critical to the development of a successful safety and health management program:

- Management leadership and employee involvement.
- Work analysis.
- Hazard prevention and control.
- Safety and health training.

The guidelines recommend specific actions, under each of these general elements, to achieve an effective safety and health program. The *Federal Register* notice is available online at www.osha.gov

State Programs

The Occupational Safety and Health Act of 1970 (OSH Act) encourages states to develop and operate their own job safety and

health plans. OSHA approves and monitors these plans. Twenty-four states, Puerto Rico and the Virgin Islands currently operate approved state plans: 23 cover both private and public (state and local government) employment; 3 states, Connecticut, New Jersey and New York, cover the public sector only. States and territories with their own OSHA-approved occupational safety and health plans must adopt standards identical to, or at least as effective as, the Federal standards.

Consultation Services

Consultation assistance is available on request to employers who want help in establishing and maintaining a safe and healthful workplace. Largely funded by OSHA, the service is provided at no cost to the employer. Primarily developed for smaller employers with more hazardous operations, the consultation service is delivered by state governments employing professional safety and health consultants. Comprehensive assistance includes an appraisal of all mechanical systems, work practices and occupational safety and health hazards of the workplace and all aspects of the employer's present job safety and health program. In addition, the service offers assistance to employers in developing and implementing an effective safety and health program. No penalties are proposed or citations issued for hazards identified by the consultant. OSHA provides consultation assistance to the employer with the assurance that his or her name and firm and any information about the workplace will not be routinely reported to OSHA enforcement staff.

Under the consultation program, certain exemplary employers may request participation in OSHA's Safety and Health Achievement Recognition Program (SHARP). Eligibility for participation in SHARP includes receiving a comprehensive consultation visit, demonstrating exemplary achievements in workplace safety and health by abating all identified hazards and developing an excellent safety and health program.

Employers accepted into SHARP may receive an exemption from programmed inspections (not complaint or accident investigation inspections) for a period of one year. For more information concerning consultation assistance, see the OSHA website at www.osha.gov

Voluntary Protection Programs (VPP)

Voluntary Protection Programs and on-site consultation services, when coupled with an effective enforcement program, expand worker protection to help meet the goals of the *OSH Act.* The three levels of VPP are Star, Merit, and Demonstration designed to recognize outstanding achievements by companies that have successfully incorporated comprehensive safety and health programs into their total management system. The VPPs motivate others to achieve excellent safety and health results in the same outstanding way as they establish a cooperative relationship between employers, employees and OSHA.

For additional information on VPP and how to apply, contact the OSHA regional offices listed at the end of this publication.

Strategic Partnership Program

OSHA's Strategic Partnership Program, the newest member of OSHA's cooperative programs, helps encourage, assist and recognize the efforts of partners to eliminate serious workplace hazards and achieve a high level of worker safety and health. Whereas OSHA's Consultation Program and VPP entail one-on-one relationships between OSHA and individual worksites, most strategic partnerships seek to have a broader impact by building cooperative relationships with groups of employers and employees. These partnerships are voluntary, cooperative relationships between OSHA, employers, employee representatives and others (e.g., trade unions, trade and professional associations, universities and other government agencies).

For more information on this and other cooperative programs, contact your nearest OSHA office, or visit OSHA's website at www.osha.gov

Alliance Programs

The Alliances Program enables organizations committed to workplace safety and health to collaborate with OSHA to prevent injuries and illnesses in the workplace. OSHA and the Alliance participants work together to reach out to, educate and lead the nation's employers and their employees in improving and advancing workplace safety and health.

Groups that can form an Alliance with OSHA include employers, labor unions, trade or professional groups and educational institutions. In some cases, organizations may be building on existing relationships with OSHA that were developed through other cooperative programs.

There are few formal program requirements for Alliances and the agreements do not include an enforcement component. However, OSHA and the participating organizations must define, implement and meet a set of short- and long-term goals that fall into three categories: training and education; outreach and communication; and promoting the national dialogue on workplace safety and health.

OSHA Training and Education

OSHA area offices offer a variety of information services, such as compliance assistance, technical advice, publications, audiovisual aids and speakers for special engagements. OSHA's Training Institute in Arlington Heights, IL, provides basic and advanced courses in safety and health for Federal and state compliance officers, state consultants, Federal agency personnel, and private sector employers, employees and their representatives.

The OSHA Training Institute also has established OSHA Training Institute Education Centers to address the increased demand for its courses from the private sector and from other Federal agencies. These centers are nonprofit colleges, universities and other organizations that have been selected after a competition for participation in the program.

OSHA also provides funds to nonprofit organizations, through grants, to conduct workplace training and education in subjects where OSHA believes there is a lack of workplace training. Grants are awarded annually. Grant recipients are expected to contribute 20 percent of the total grant cost.

For more information on grants, training and education, contact the OSHA Training Institute, Office of Training and Education, 2020 South Arlington Heights Road, Arlington Heights, IL 60005, (847) 297-4810 or see "Outreach" on OSHA's website at www.osha.gov. For further information on any OSHA program, contact your nearest OSHA area or regional office listed at the end of this publication.

Information Available Electronically

OSHA has a variety of materials and tools available on its website at www.osha.gov. These include *e-Tools* such as *Expert Advisors, Electronic Compliance Assistance Tools (e-cats), Technical Links*; regulations, directives and publications; videos and other information for employers and employees. OSHA's software programs and compliance assistance tools walk you through challenging safety and health issues and common problems to find the best solutions for your workplace.

A wide variety of OSHA materials, including standards, interpretations, directives, and more, can be purchased on CD-ROM from the U.S. Government Printing Office, Superintendent of Documents, phone toll-free (866) 512-1800.

OSHA Publications

OSHA has an extensive publications program. For a listing of free or sales items, visit OSHA's website at www.osha.gov or contact the OSHA Publications Office, U.S. Department of Labor, 200 Constitution Avenue, NW, N-3101, Washington, DC 20210. Telephone (202) 693-1888 or fax to (202) 693-2498.

Contacting OSHA

To report an emergency, file a complaint or seek OSHA advice, assistance or products, call (800) 321-OSHA or contact your nearest OSHA regional or area office listed at the end of this publication. The teletypewriter (TTY) number is (877) 889-5627.

You can also file a complaint online and obtain more information on OSHA Federal and state programs by visiting OSHA's website at www.osha.gov

OSHA Regional Offices

Region I
(CT,* ME, MA, NH, RI, VT*)
JFK Federal Building, Room E340
Boston, MA 02203
(617) 565-9860

Region II
(NJ,* NY,* PR,* VI*)
201 Varick Street, Room 670
New York, NY 10014
(212) 337-2378

Region III
(DE, DC, MD,* PA, VA,* WV)
The Curtis Center
170 S. Independence Mall West
Suite 740 West
Philadelphia, PA 19106-3309
(215) 861-4900

Region IV
(AL, FL, GA, KY,* MS, NC,* SC,* TN*)
61 Forsyth Street, SW
Atlanta, GA 30303
(404) 562-2300

Region V
(IL, IN,* MI,* MN,* OH, WI)
230 South Dearborn Street
Room 3244
Chicago, IL 60604
(312) 353-2220

Region VI
(AR, LA, NM,* OK, TX)
525 Griffin Street, Room 602
Dallas, TX 75202
(214) 767-4731 or 4736 x224

Region VII
(IA,* KS, MO, NE)
City Center Square
1100 Main Street, Suite 800
Kansas City, MO 64105
(816) 426-5861

Region VIII
(CO, MT, ND, SD, UT,* WY*)
1999 Broadway, Suite 1690
PO Box 46550
Denver, CO 80202-5716
(720) 264-6550

Region IX
(American Samoa, AZ,* CA,* HI,* NV,*
Northern Mariana Islands)
71 Stevenson Street, Room 420
San Francisco, CA 94105
(415) 975-4310

Region X
(AK,* ID, OR,* WA*)
1111 Third Avenue, Suite 715
Seattle, WA 98101-3212
(206) 553-5930

* These states and territories operate their own OSHA-approved job safety and health programs (Connecticut, New Jersey and New York plans cover public employees only). States with approved programs must have a standard that is identical to, or at least as effective as, the Federal standard.

Note: To get contact information for OSHA Area Offices, OSHA-approved State Plans and OSHA Consultation Projects, please visit us online at www.osha.gov or call us at 1-800-321-OSHA.

www.ingramcontent.com/pod-product-compliance
Lightning Source LLC
Chambersburg PA
CBHW051828170526
45167CB00005B/2205